ROSEN ✓ Verified
U.S. GOVERNMENT

ELECTING A U.S. PRESIDENT

Xina M. Uhl

ROSEN
PUBLISHING

New York

T0018489

Published in 2021 by The Rosen Publishing Group, Inc.
29 East 21st Street, New York, NY 10010

Editor: Siyavush Saidian
Book Design: Reann Nye

Photo Credits: Cover Hill Street Studios/DigitalVision/Getty Images; series Art PinkPueblo/Shutterstock .com; p. 5 Tyler Burns/Shutterstock.com; p. 7 (top) Mikhail Kolesnikov/Shutterstock.com; p. 7 (middle) Miljan Mladenovic/Shutterstock.com; p. 7 (bottom) Steven Frame/Shutterstock.com; p. 9 https:// commons.wikimedia.org/wiki/File:Gilbert_Stuart_Williamstown_Portrait_of_George_Washington.jpg; p. 10 Nerthuz/Shutterstock.com; pp. 11, 23 (map) Maps Expert/Shutterstock.com; p. 13 JEFF KOWALSKY/ AFP/Getty Images News/Getty Images; p. 15 adamkaz/E+/Getty Images; p. 17 Atstock Productions/ Shutterstock.com; p. 19 Jim Cole/AP Images; p. 20 Sean Rayford/Getty Images News/Getty Images; p. 21 NurPhoto/Getty Images; p. 23 (button) bearsky23/Shutterstock.com; pp. 25, 39 Mark Makela/ Getty Images News/Getty Images; p. 27 Joe Raedle/Getty Images News/Getty Images; p. 29 AFP/ Getty Images; p. 31 Rob Crandall/Shutterstock.com; p. 33 Robert Daemmrich Photography Inc/Corbis Historical/Getty Images; p. 35 DNetromphotos/Shuttertock.com; p. 37 Anadolu Agency/Getty Images; p. 41 Henry Guttmann Collection/Hulton Archive/Getty Images; p. 43 Bloomberg/Getty Images; p. 45 Sean Locke Photography/Shutterstock.com.

Library of Congress Cataloging-in-Publication Data

Names: Uhl, Xina M., author. | Rosen Publishing Group.
Title: Electing a U.S. president / Xina M. Uhl.
Other titles: Electing a United States president
Description: New York : Rosen Publishing, 2021. | Series: Rosen Verified:
    U.S. Government | Includes index.
Identifiers: LCCN 2019060008 | ISBN 9781499468557 (Library Binding) | ISBN
    9781499468540 (Paperback)
Subjects: LCSH: Presidents—United States—Election—Juvenile literature. |
    Elections—United States—Juvenile literature. | Electoral
    college—United States—Juvenile literature. | Political
    conventions—United States—Juvenile literature. | Primaries—United
    States—Juvenile literature. | United States—Politics and
    government—Juvenile literature.
Classification: LCC JK528 .U47 2021 | DDC 324.973—dc23
LC record available at https://lccn.loc.gov/2019060008

Manufactured in the United States of America

Some of the images in this book illustrate individuals who are models. The depictions do not imply actual situations or events.

CPSIA Compliance Information: Batch #BSR20. For Further Information contact Rosen Publishing, New York, New York at 1-800-237-9932.

Find us on

CONTENTS

THE NUMBER—ONE JOB

If there's one job that everyone in the United States knows about, it's the U.S. presidency. The person who holds this office is on the news constantly. Their face is known across both the United States and the world. But how does this person get their job?

The Constitution is the basis of the U.S. government. Article II, Section 1 describes what the president does and who can hold office. A president's term lasts four years. The 22nd **Amendment** says a person can't be elected more than twice. The president must be a citizen born in the United States. They can't be younger than 35. Meeting these qualifications is just the first step. To win the presidency, someone has to **campaign**.

On Mount Rushmore in South Dakota, four U.S. presidents are set in stone. The presidents, from left to right, are George Washington, Thomas Jefferson, Theodore Roosevelt, and Abraham Lincoln.

THE THREE BRANCHES

The U.S. Constitution went into effect in 1789. Ever since, it has served as the basis for the country's laws. The government has three parts, each with its own duties.

• The legislative branch makes laws. The Senate and House of Representatives are in this branch.

• The executive branch carries out laws. This branch consists of the president, vice president, and cabinet.

• The judicial branch is made up of the Supreme Court and other federal courts. This branch makes sure laws follow the Constitution.

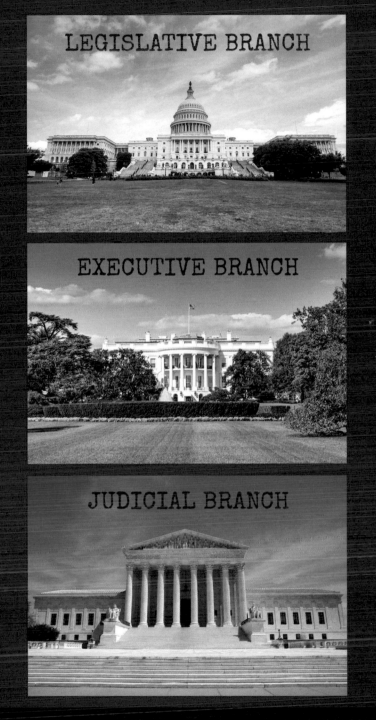

LEGISLATIVE BRANCH

EXECUTIVE BRANCH

JUDICIAL BRANCH

✓ VERIFIED

The U.S. government is divided into three branches. Each branch's duties are limited. This is done so that one branch doesn't become more powerful than the others. Its website is:
https://www.usa.gov/branches-of-government

THE JOB DESCRIPTION

As head of the executive branch, the president has many duties. Their main duty is to approve bills from Congress. A bill must be approved or **vetoed** within 10 days. When a bill is approved, it becomes a law. If a bill is vetoed, Congress can override it with enough votes. Otherwise, it won't become a law.

The president can decide to pardon people. Another duty is to command the country's military. The president also deals with foreign countries. He or she appoints ambassadors and makes treaties.

A president can be removed from office. First, the House of Representatives must **impeach** them. If the president is found guilty of the charges in the trial held in the Senate, then they'll lose their job.

George Washington was the nation's first president. His term lasted from 1789 to 1797.

THE FIRST PRESIDENT

During the American Revolution, George Washington served as general. His talents earned him respect and fame. He was chosen to lead the meeting at which the Constitution was created. Washington's fellow **delegates** wanted him to be president. He agreed to take the job, even though he wanted to retire.

POLITICAL PARTIES

A political party is a group of people with similar ideas about government and what it should do. The United States has two major political parties. These are the Democratic Party and the Republican Party. Each has different beliefs and is known by different colors. The Democratic color is blue. The Republican color is red. The president typically represents one of these parties. That party helps to get their **candidate** elected.

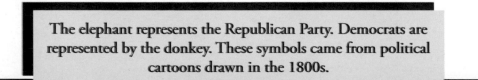

The elephant represents the Republican Party. Democrats are represented by the donkey. These symbols came from political cartoons drawn in the 1800s.

WHAT WASHINGTON THOUGHT

The country's first president, George Washington, didn't like political parties. He thought they divided the country. He worried division would destroy the United States. Even though he warned against them, parties are a major part of politics.

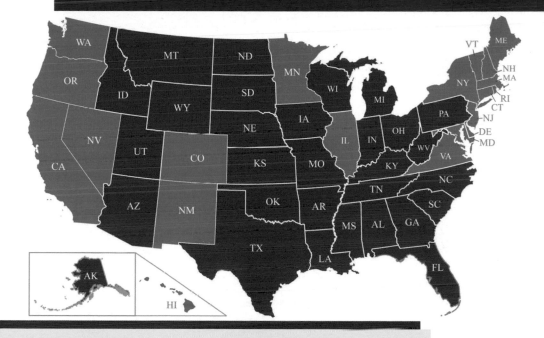

Count the red states (Republican) and the blue states (Democrat) on this 2016 election map. How did your state vote?

Democrats often favor giving less money to the military. Republicans favor giving the military more money. Democrats tend to support more taxes. Republicans do not. The two parties have many other differences.

Other parties exist, such as the Green Party. The Libertarian Party is another. However, these parties are small and don't have much power.

A BIG DECISION

The decision to run for president might be easy. The current president, or incumbent, may want another term. If the incumbent can run again, their political party usually supports them.

For others, the decision can be hard. Running for president is challenging. It takes a lot of time and energy. Despite the difficulties, many people want the job.

HOW TO RUN

The first steps for a presidential candidate are:

1. Fill out a form called a statement of candidacy.

2. Get on the **ballot** in each state. This means the candidate's name will appear in state elections. Voters use ballots to mark whom they're voting for. They can be paper or electronic.

3. Get a team of people to help. Most members of the team are volunteers. They agree with the candidate's ideas.

A ballot, like the one shown here, has a list of names, the candidate's party, and a place for voters to mark their choice. This is the type of ballot often used at polling places.

WHAT CANDIDATES STAND FOR

People who run for president take **positions** about their beliefs. Some positions involve how to bring new jobs to the country. Others are about taxes, health care, and the military. Crime is often a concern. So are the environment and education.

Candidates try to say what voters want to hear. They try to show how different they are from each other. They want to appeal to as many people as they can. Their ideas lead to promises for what they'll work on if they're elected.

✓ VERIFIED

It takes a lot of work to run for president. You can find a rundown of what's required here: **https://www.usa.gov/election**

Candidates for president must think about many groups of Americans. Older Americans often like candidates who support Social Security payments and Medicare services.

A TEAM OF HELPERS

A person cannot run for president alone. It takes a whole team of people. This is because there are a lot of tasks to do. Raising money is a big job because campaigns cost a lot. Money pays for ads, signs, travel, and more. Volunteers who help with a president's campaign spend a lot of time asking for donations.

Volunteers live in every state. They take time from their lives to help their candidate. There are some paid positions in campaigns. For Joe Biden's 2020 campaign, he had 11 paid staff members.

The team also helps the candidate appeal to the public. This means helping the candidate get support from unions and other groups.

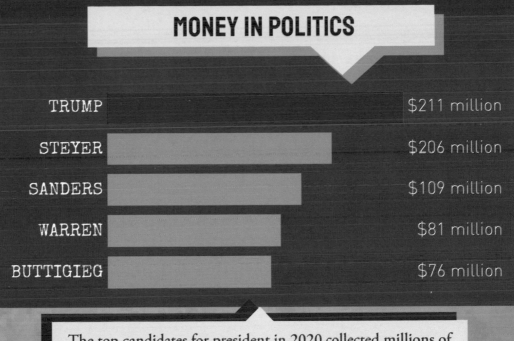

MONEY IN POLITICS

Candidate	Amount
TRUMP	$211 million
STEYER	$206 million
SANDERS	$109 million
WARREN	$81 million
BUTTIGIEG	$76 million

The top candidates for president in 2020 collected millions of dollars to pay for their campaigns.

Volunteers gather to figure out how to promote their candidate. They work to answer questions and give people details about the candidate and their positions.

GETTING THE WORD OUT

Candidates need the support of their political party and its voters if they hope to win. They try to get attention for themselves in different ways:

• RALLIES

A **rally** is a special event held to get people excited about a candidate. At a rally, candidates give speeches about their ideas.

• PRESS COVERAGE

A candidate gives interviews to the news media. Many people see these online or read about them in newspapers.

• SOCIAL MEDIA

Candidates use Twitter, Facebook, and other social media to talk about their beliefs. During the 2016 election, President Trump used his Twitter account to gain a lot of support.

• VISITS

Candidates visit voters in person. During his 2012 campaign for reelection, President Obama stopped by a number of restaurants. There, he met people and talked about his ideas.

President Obama visited restaurants and stores around the country during his first campaign for president. Candidates like to show that they're one of the people.

HOLDING DEBATES

Candidates for president often join **debates**. These are events that feature several candidates on a stage. They are held in front of an audience. People can also watch on TV. The candidates answer questions about their plans. They often disagree with one another.

Democratic presidential candidate Senator Elizabeth Warren is shown here on stage answering audience questions.

OPINION POLLS

One way that campaigns measure how well they're doing is through polls. A poll involves asking a sample of people how they plan to vote. Their responses are recorded. **Pollsters** then predict how many votes each candidate will get. The numbers are given as percentages. It's important to remember one thing about polls: they're only predictions.

Polls predicted that Hillary Clinton would win the 2016 election. She lost to Donald Trump.

At the start of an election, the Democratic and Republican Parties might hold debates between their candidates. The final debates of an election are between just two candidates.

PRIMARY OR CAUCUS?

When a political party has a number of candidates, it has to narrow the field. This means that it has to decide which person to support. The top candidate is found through one of two ways, depending on the state: **primary** or **caucus**.

PRIMARY

This is an election held in certain states. Voters use ballots to choose a candidate they like best.

CAUCUS

This is a meeting. People vote for candidates by raising their hands. They may also break into groups and cast their votes that way.

✓ VERIFIED

You can learn more about the history behind caucuses and primaries here:
https://www.factcheck.org/2008/04/ caucus-vs-primary

SUPER TUESDAY

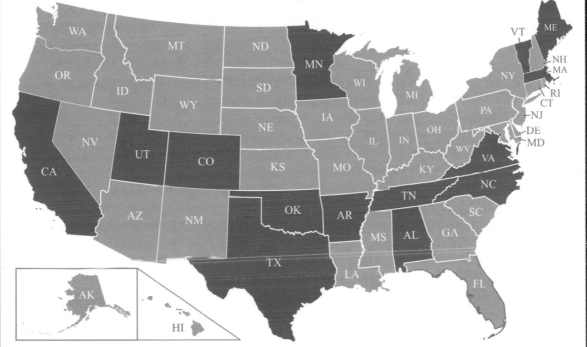

Super Tuesday occurs in each presidential election year. It is the Tuesday when a large number of states hold their primary elections. The map above shows which states will hold primaries on Super Tuesday in 2020.

CHOOSING A NOMINEE

Once all the states' primaries and caucuses are held, the numbers are added up. Each political party sees which candidate got the most votes. That person will become the party's **nominee** for president.

Two special events are held the summer before the election. Called national conventions, the Democratic and Republican Parties each host one. They're attended by hundreds of delegates. They represent the voters of each state. They promise to cast a vote that represents what their voters want.

At the national convention, the nominee makes speeches. The people who attend get excited. Sometimes, conventions also have entertainment, like concerts.

While the two major parties' conventions are the biggest, they aren't the only ones. The Libertarian Party holds a convention. So does the Green Party. Others might as well. These events are much smaller.

Donald Trump was the Republican nominee for president in 2016. After the convention, he was the only Republican candidate for president in the upcoming election.

RUNNING AS ONE

Candidates for president need to pick a running mate. This person will serve as vice president if they win. The two of them campaign together.

Candidates must be careful to choose a good running mate. Voters may like the candidate but not their chosen vice president. In these cases, their votes may go to someone else.

WHAT DOES THE VICE PRESIDENT DO?

The main job of the vice president is to take over the job of president if needed. The president may get sick. They may even die in office. With this system, there will always be a president.

The vice president also serves as president of the Senate. They can cast a vote if there's a tie.

Donald Trump chose Mike Pence as his running mate during the 2016 election. Pence was the governor of Indiana from 2013 to 2017.

TALKING AND MORE TALKING

After the political conventions are held, more debates take place. These include two presidential debates. There's also one debate between the running mates. The debates are only between two people. These are the Democratic and Republican nominees. Even though they're not present at the debates, candidates for smaller political parties will still run for president.

Most of the time, these debates are held at colleges. News anchors often **moderate** them. Each candidate is asked certain questions. They have a limited amount of time to answer. This is a chance for each candidate to show how their ideas are different or better.

The general election presidential debates are between two people, unlike the earlier debates. Here, Hillary Clinton and Donald Trump debate during the 2016 campaign.

WHAT CANDIDATES SAY

Candidates can be asked all kinds of questions at debates. Hillary Clinton spoke about the Supreme Court during the final debate of the 2016 presidential race:

"The Supreme Court should represent all of us. That's how I see the court, and the kind of people that I would be looking to nominate to the court would be in the great tradition of standing up to the powerful, standing up on behalf of our rights as Americans."

ELECTION DAY

The presidential election happens every four years. Election Day is always on the first Tuesday after the first Monday of November. **Absentee** voters mail their votes in before this. Some states have only mail-in ballots.

In most states, people cast their votes at their local polling place. They first check in at a desk. Next, they go to a voting booth, where they cast their votes. The booth keeps others from seeing a voter's choices.

Polling places are often schools and churches. The place can be a government building or store too. The building must be easy to get to. It must also meet certain standards by law.

Polling places usually stay open all day. The polling places close at varying times in different states. The last states to close are on the West Coast due to the time zone. Final votes are counted after this.

The Constitution says that voters must have a secret ballot. This keeps other people from seeing how someone votes.

✓ VERIFIED

Your polling location may be closer than you think!
Check out this locator to find out where you can vote:
https://www.vote.org/polling-place-locator

IS THE ELECTORAL COLLEGE A SCHOOL?

Most elections are settled by popular vote. This means that the person who gets the most votes wins. That's not how presidential elections are held. The Constitution sets up a system called the Electoral College. Despite its name, this is not a place. It's a group of people.

ELECTORAL STEPS

The Electoral College follows a process that can be split into three steps:

• The first is choosing the **electors**. Political parties choose people to be electors. When a person votes, they're making a choice to select the state's electors.

• The second is for electors to cast votes. Electors are supposed to vote for the candidate chosen by their state. As representatives, they have a duty to follow the wishes of the voters where they live. They can vote for someone else. This almost never happens, though.

• The third step in the electoral process is for Congress to count the electoral votes. These votes decide the outcome of the election.

Political parties pick loyal supporters to be electors. They want to reward these supporters for helping the party.

NUMBERS AND THE ELECTORAL COLLEGE

Numbers are important in the Electoral College. On election night, campaign workers watch the following numbers carefully. So do the news media and voters.

ELECTORAL STEPS

- There are 538 electors. Each state has as many electors as they do members of Congress.

- To win as president, that candidate must have at least 270 electoral votes. This is more than half of the total votes.

- Every 10 years, the number of a state's electoral votes is updated. This keeps it up to date with changes in Congress.

✔ VERIFIED

You can read more about the electoral college in this article from the National Archives:
https://www.archives.gov/electoral-college/about

FAITHLESS ELECTORS

A faithless elector is one who doesn't cast their vote for the candidate their state's voters chose. This happened in elections in 1948, 1956, 1960, 1968, 1972, 1976, and 1988. These electors claim they had a good reason for what they did. They said they voted their conscience. In other words, they voted for what they believed.

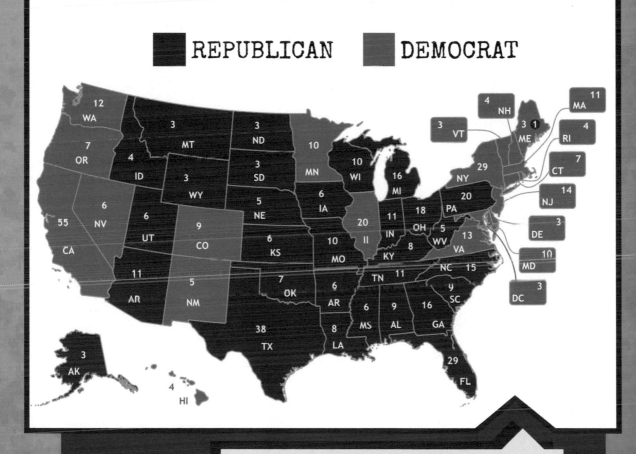

This map shows the number of electoral votes for each state in the 2016 presidential election. California has the largest number of votes due to its population.

THE POPULAR VOTE

Electoral votes aren't the same as popular votes. Electoral votes don't count every voter's personal choice. Instead, they consider only the candidate who wins in each state. Whoever wins gets all that state's electoral votes.

The popular vote is the actual number of votes cast by Americans. The winner of the popular vote doesn't always win the election. This happened in the 2016 election between Trump and Clinton. Many people believe that the candidate who wins the popular vote should win the election.

In 2016, Donald Trump got more electoral votes than Hillary Clinton. She got more popular votes, but Trump became president.

SHOULD WE KEEP THE ELECTORAL COLLEGE?

The Constitution created the Electoral College. Some people think it's outdated. They want it removed. There are arguments for and against this idea.

PRO

These are the reasons some people think the system should remain as it is:

- Electors are informed and educated. Some voters are not.

- The Electoral College gives smaller states more weight. If it didn't exist, the heavily populated areas would always decide the winner. That would leave out a lot of areas.

- The Electoral College has only several hundred votes. These are easier to keep track of than tens of millions.

- It encourages candidates to consider the concerns of people across the country.

Many people were unhappy with Trump's election. Some of them protested against him.

AGAINST THE ELECTORAL COLLEGE

CONS

These are the reasons some people think the system should change:

• The Electoral College is out of date. Computers didn't exist when the country was founded. They can now be used to count votes.

• Some states get too much power. They're called swing states. Swing states can side with either party. Other states almost always vote for a certain party and any other votes don't make a difference.

• By choosing the president based on the popular vote, individual people have a greater say in politics.

QUICK QUESTION

What do you think? Should the Electoral College stay or go?

The House of Representatives has chosen the president only twice. Once was in 1800 with Thomas Jefferson. The second time was in 1824, when John Quincy Adams won.

SPECIAL CASES

Rarely, neither candidate wins the majority of electoral votes. What happens then? The House of Representatives steps in. They cast votes for one of the top three candidates. The winner becomes president. The Senate picks the vice president from the other two candidates.

VICTORY OR DEFEAT

After the presidential election, votes are counted quickly. Most of the time, counting a small number of votes shows who won that state. This is known as calling the state for one candidate or another. When the vote is close in a state, it cannot be called until enough votes are counted.

When the winner is clear, that person gives a victory speech. Then they hold a party to celebrate. The loser gives a **concession** speech. That person thanks their supporters for their work.

During Donald Trump's 2016 victory speech, he shared the stage with his family. He promised to do his best to lead the country.

THE LONG PROCESS

Electing a president is a long process. It takes about two years from start to finish. There are a lot of candidates at the start. That number gets narrowed down over time. At the end, only one person represents each party.

Political parties play a big role in these elections. So do the voters. They have a duty to watch debates and learn about the candidates before they vote.

The Electoral College determines the winner of the presidency. Some people debate about whether it should still exist.

Elections mostly go smoothly. The Constitution guides actions when it doesn't. The U.S. government is committed to giving voters a choice about whom they want as president. One day, you can make that choice yourself.

When Election Day comes, the person with the most electoral votes gets to be president. The U.S. electoral process has its critics. Until a Constitutional amendment changes it, though, the process will remain.

GLOSSARY

absentee: A person who cannot be present for an event.

amendment: A change in the words or meaning of a law or document, such as a constitution.

ballot: A means to cast a vote.

campaign: A series of activities to bring about a goal, such as an election.

candidate: A person who runs in an election.

caucus: A meeting held by a political party to select a candidate.

concession: An admission of defeat.

debate: A discussion between two sides.

delegate: A representative.

elector: A member of the Electoral College, which is the group that elects the president and vice president of the United States.

impeach: To charge an elected official with a crime done while in office.

moderate: To guide a discussion.

nominee: A person whom a group supports for an elected position.

pollster: A person who collects data.

position: A stand on a question.

primary: An election in which members of the same political party run against each other for the chance to be in a larger and more important election.

rally: An event to get people excited.

veto: An action which prevents a bill from becoming a law.

INDEX